DATE

TIME

LOCATION

ENVIRONMENT

☐ FOREST	☐ GRASSLAND
☐ DESERT	☐ TUNDRA
☐ FRESHWATER	☐ MARINE

TYPE

SHAPE

WEIGHT

LENGTH	WIDTH	DEPTH

COLORS

TEXTURE

LUSTER

EQUIPMENT

-
-
-

SETTINGS

EXTENDED DESCRIPTION

DATE

TIME

LOCATION

ENVIRONMENT

☐ FOREST	☐ GRASSLAND
☐ DESERT	☐ TUNDRA
☐ FRESHWATER	☐ MARINE

TYPE

SHAPE

WEIGHT

COLORS

TEXTURE

LUSTER

SKETCH / SAMPLE

LENGTH	WIDTH	DEPTH

EQUIPMENT

-
-
-

SETTINGS

EXTENDED DESCRIPTION

DATE

TIME

LOCATION

ENVIRONMENT

☐ FOREST	☐ GRASSLAND
☐ DESERT	☐ TUNDRA
☐ FRESHWATER	☐ MARINE

TYPE

SHAPE

WEIGHT

COLORS

TEXTURE

LUSTER

SKETCH / SAMPLE

LENGTH	WIDTH	DEPTH

EQUIPMENT

-
-
-

SETTINGS

EXTENDED DESCRIPTION

DATE

TIME

LOCATION

ENVIRONMENT

☐ FOREST	☐ GRASSLAND
☐ DESERT	☐ TUNDRA
☐ FRESHWATER	☐ MARINE

TYPE

SHAPE

WEIGHT

COLORS

TEXTURE

LUSTER

SKETCH / SAMPLE

LENGTH	WIDTH	DEPTH

EQUIPMENT

-
-
-

SETTINGS

EXTENDED DESCRIPTION

DATE

TIME

LOCATION

ENVIRONMENT

☐ FOREST	☐ GRASSLAND
☐ DESERT	☐ TUNDRA
☐ FRESHWATER	☐ MARINE

TYPE

SHAPE

WEIGHT

COLORS

TEXTURE

LUSTER

SKETCH / SAMPLE

LENGTH	WIDTH	DEPTH

EQUIPMENT

-
-
-

SETTINGS

EXTENDED DESCRIPTION

DATE

TIME

LOCATION

ENVIRONMENT

☐ FOREST	☐ GRASSLAND
☐ DESERT	☐ TUNDRA
☐ FRESHWATER	☐ MARINE

TYPE

SHAPE

WEIGHT

COLORS

TEXTURE

LUSTER

SKETCH / SAMPLE

LENGTH	WIDTH	DEPTH

EQUIPMENT

-
-
-

SETTINGS

EXTENDED DESCRIPTION

DATE	
TIME	
LOCATION	

ENVIRONMENT

☐ FOREST	☐ GRASSLAND
☐ DESERT	☐ TUNDRA
☐ FRESHWATER	☐ MARINE

TYPE	
SHAPE	
WEIGHT	

| COLORS |
| |
| TEXTURE |
| |
| LUSTER |
| |

SKETCH / SAMPLE

LENGTH	WIDTH	DEPTH

EQUIPMENT

-
-
-

SETTINGS

EXTENDED DESCRIPTION

DATE

TIME

LOCATION

ENVIRONMENT

☐ FOREST	☐ GRASSLAND
☐ DESERT	☐ TUNDRA
☐ FRESHWATER	☐ MARINE

TYPE

SHAPE

WEIGHT

COLORS

TEXTURE

LUSTER

SKETCH / SAMPLE

LENGTH	WIDTH	DEPTH

EQUIPMENT

-
-
-

SETTINGS

EXTENDED DESCRIPTION

DATE	SKETCH / SAMPLE
TIME	
LOCATION	

ENVIRONMENT

☐ FOREST	☐ GRASSLAND
☐ DESERT	☐ TUNDRA
☐ FRESHWATER	☐ MARINE

- TYPE
- SHAPE
- WEIGHT

LENGTH	WIDTH	DEPTH

COLORS

TEXTURE

LUSTER

EQUIPMENT

- •
- •
- •
- SETTINGS

EXTENDED DESCRIPTION

DATE

TIME

LOCATION

ENVIRONMENT

☐ FOREST	☐ GRASSLAND
☐ DESERT	☐ TUNDRA
☐ FRESHWATER	☐ MARINE

TYPE

SHAPE

WEIGHT

COLORS

TEXTURE

LUSTER

SKETCH / SAMPLE

LENGTH	WIDTH	DEPTH

EQUIPMENT

-
-
-

SETTINGS

EXTENDED DESCRIPTION

DATE

TIME

LOCATION

ENVIRONMENT

☐ FOREST	☐ GRASSLAND
☐ DESERT	☐ TUNDRA
☐ FRESHWATER	☐ MARINE

TYPE

SHAPE

WEIGHT

SKETCH / SAMPLE

LENGTH	WIDTH	DEPTH

COLORS

TEXTURE

LUSTER

EQUIPMENT

-
-
-

SETTINGS

EXTENDED DESCRIPTION

DATE		SKETCH / SAMPLE

DATE

TIME

LOCATION

ENVIRONMENT

☐ FOREST	☐ GRASSLAND
☐ DESERT	☐ TUNDRA
☐ FRESHWATER	☐ MARINE

TYPE

SHAPE

WEIGHT

COLORS

TEXTURE

LUSTER

SKETCH / SAMPLE

LENGTH	WIDTH	DEPTH

EQUIPMENT

- •
- •
- •

SETTINGS

EXTENDED DESCRIPTION

DATE

TIME

LOCATION

ENVIRONMENT

☐ FOREST	☐ GRASSLAND
☐ DESERT	☐ TUNDRA
☐ FRESHWATER	☐ MARINE

TYPE

SHAPE

WEIGHT

COLORS

TEXTURE

LUSTER

SKETCH / SAMPLE

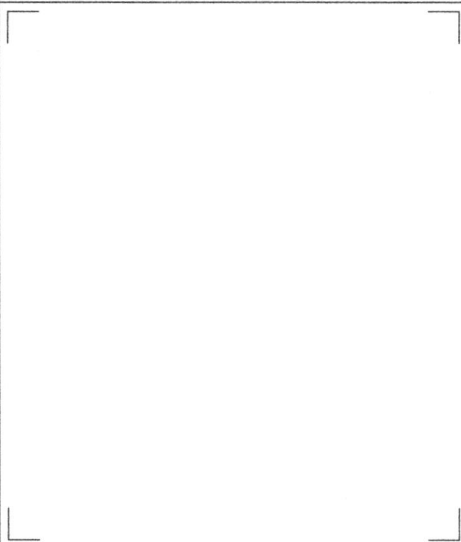

LENGTH	WIDTH	DEPTH

EQUIPMENT

-
-
-

SETTINGS

EXTENDED DESCRIPTION

DATE

TIME

LOCATION

ENVIRONMENT

☐ FOREST	☐ GRASSLAND
☐ DESERT	☐ TUNDRA
☐ FRESHWATER	☐ MARINE

TYPE

SHAPE

WEIGHT

COLORS

TEXTURE

LUSTER

SKETCH / SAMPLE

LENGTH	WIDTH	DEPTH

EQUIPMENT

-
-
-

SETTINGS

EXTENDED DESCRIPTION

📅 DATE	SKETCH / SAMPLE
🕐 TIME	
📍 LOCATION	

ENVIRONMENT

☐ FOREST	☐ GRASSLAND
☐ DESERT	☐ TUNDRA
☐ FRESHWATER	☐ MARINE

🔺 TYPE
🔻 SHAPE
⚖️ WEIGHT

LENGTH	WIDTH	DEPTH

⊕ COLORS
▨ TEXTURE
✦ LUSTER

EQUIPMENT

-
-
-

⚙ SETTINGS

EXTENDED DESCRIPTION

DATE

TIME

LOCATION

ENVIRONMENT

☐ FOREST	☐ GRASSLAND
☐ DESERT	☐ TUNDRA
☐ FRESHWATER	☐ MARINE

TYPE

SHAPE

WEIGHT

COLORS

TEXTURE

LUSTER

SKETCH / SAMPLE

LENGTH	WIDTH	DEPTH

EQUIPMENT

-
-
-

SETTINGS

EXTENDED DESCRIPTION

DATE	
TIME	
LOCATION	

ENVIRONMENT

☐ FOREST	☐ GRASSLAND
☐ DESERT	☐ TUNDRA
☐ FRESHWATER	☐ MARINE

TYPE	
SHAPE	
WEIGHT	

SKETCH / SAMPLE

LENGTH	WIDTH	DEPTH

COLORS

TEXTURE

LUSTER

EQUIPMENT

-
-
-

SETTINGS

EXTENDED DESCRIPTION

📅 **DATE**	
🕐 **TIME**	
📍 **LOCATION**	

ENVIRONMENT

- [ ] FOREST
- [ ] GRASSLAND
- [ ] DESERT
- [ ] TUNDRA
- [ ] FRESHWATER
- [ ] MARINE

◆ **TYPE**

▽ **SHAPE**

⚖ **WEIGHT**

SKETCH / SAMPLE

LENGTH	WIDTH	DEPTH

◎ **COLORS**

▨ **TEXTURE**

✦ **LUSTER**

EQUIPMENT

- •
- •
- •

≡ SETTINGS

EXTENDED DESCRIPTION

DATE

TIME

LOCATION

ENVIRONMENT

☐ FOREST	☐ GRASSLAND
☐ DESERT	☐ TUNDRA
☐ FRESHWATER	☐ MARINE

TYPE

SHAPE

WEIGHT

COLORS

TEXTURE

LUSTER

SKETCH / SAMPLE

LENGTH	WIDTH	DEPTH

EQUIPMENT

-
-
-

SETTINGS

EXTENDED DESCRIPTION

DATE

TIME

LOCATION

ENVIRONMENT

☐ FOREST	☐ GRASSLAND
☐ DESERT	☐ TUNDRA
☐ FRESHWATER	☐ MARINE

TYPE

SHAPE

WEIGHT

COLORS

TEXTURE

LUSTER

SKETCH / SAMPLE

LENGTH	WIDTH	DEPTH

EQUIPMENT

-
-
-

SETTINGS

EXTENDED DESCRIPTION

DATE	SKETCH / SAMPLE
TIME	
LOCATION	

ENVIRONMENT

FOREST	GRASSLAND
DESERT	TUNDRA
FRESHWATER	MARINE

TYPE

SHAPE

WEIGHT

LENGTH	WIDTH	DEPTH

COLORS

TEXTURE

LUSTER

EQUIPMENT

-
-
-

SETTINGS

EXTENDED DESCRIPTION

DATE

TIME

LOCATION

ENVIRONMENT

☐ FOREST	☐ GRASSLAND
☐ DESERT	☐ TUNDRA
☐ FRESHWATER	☐ MARINE

TYPE

SHAPE

WEIGHT

COLORS

TEXTURE

LUSTER

SKETCH / SAMPLE

LENGTH	WIDTH	DEPTH

EQUIPMENT

-
-
-

SETTINGS

EXTENDED DESCRIPTION

DATE

TIME

LOCATION

ENVIRONMENT

☐ FOREST	☐ GRASSLAND
☐ DESERT	☐ TUNDRA
☐ FRESHWATER	☐ MARINE

TYPE

SHAPE

WEIGHT

COLORS

TEXTURE

LUSTER

SKETCH / SAMPLE

LENGTH	WIDTH	DEPTH

EQUIPMENT

-
-
-

SETTINGS

EXTENDED DESCRIPTION

DATE	SKETCH / SAMPLE
TIME	
LOCATION	

ENVIRONMENT

☐ FOREST	☐ GRASSLAND
☐ DESERT	☐ TUNDRA
☐ FRESHWATER	☐ MARINE

TYPE
SHAPE
WEIGHT

LENGTH	WIDTH	DEPTH

COLORS
TEXTURE
LUSTER

EQUIPMENT

-
-
-

SETTINGS

EXTENDED DESCRIPTION

DATE		SKETCH / SAMPLE

DATE

TIME

LOCATION

ENVIRONMENT

☐ FOREST	☐ GRASSLAND
☐ DESERT	☐ TUNDRA
☐ FRESHWATER	☐ MARINE

TYPE

SHAPE

WEIGHT

COLORS

TEXTURE

LUSTER

SKETCH / SAMPLE

LENGTH	WIDTH	DEPTH

EQUIPMENT

-
-
-

SETTINGS

EXTENDED DESCRIPTION

DATE

TIME

LOCATION

ENVIRONMENT

☐ FOREST	☐ GRASSLAND
☐ DESERT	☐ TUNDRA
☐ FRESHWATER	☐ MARINE

TYPE

SHAPE

WEIGHT

COLORS

TEXTURE

LUSTER

SKETCH / SAMPLE

LENGTH	WIDTH	DEPTH

EQUIPMENT

-
-
-

SETTINGS

EXTENDED DESCRIPTION

DATE

TIME

LOCATION

ENVIRONMENT

☐ FOREST	☐ GRASSLAND
☐ DESERT	☐ TUNDRA
☐ FRESHWATER	☐ MARINE

TYPE

SHAPE

WEIGHT

COLORS

TEXTURE

LUSTER

SKETCH / SAMPLE

LENGTH	WIDTH	DEPTH

EQUIPMENT

-
-
-

SETTINGS

EXTENDED DESCRIPTION

DATE	
TIME	
LOCATION	

SKETCH / SAMPLE

LENGTH	WIDTH	DEPTH

ENVIRONMENT

☐ FOREST	☐ GRASSLAND
☐ DESERT	☐ TUNDRA
☐ FRESHWATER	☐ MARINE

TYPE	
SHAPE	
WEIGHT	

COLORS

TEXTURE

LUSTER

EQUIPMENT

-
-
-

SETTINGS

EXTENDED DESCRIPTION

📅 **DATE**
🕐 **TIME**
📍 **LOCATION**

ENVIRONMENT

☐ FOREST	☐ GRASSLAND
☐ DESERT	☐ TUNDRA
☐ FRESHWATER	☐ MARINE

🔺 **TYPE**
🔻 **SHAPE**
⚖️ **WEIGHT**

SKETCH / SAMPLE

LENGTH	WIDTH	DEPTH

⬤ **COLORS**
▧ **TEXTURE**
✦ **LUSTER**

EQUIPMENT

-
-
-

⚙ SETTINGS

EXTENDED DESCRIPTION

DATE

TIME

LOCATION

ENVIRONMENT

☐ FOREST	☐ GRASSLAND
☐ DESERT	☐ TUNDRA
☐ FRESHWATER	☐ MARINE

TYPE

SHAPE

WEIGHT

COLORS

TEXTURE

LUSTER

SKETCH / SAMPLE

LENGTH	WIDTH	DEPTH

EQUIPMENT

-
-
-

SETTINGS

EXTENDED DESCRIPTION

DATE

TIME

LOCATION

ENVIRONMENT

☐ FOREST	☐ GRASSLAND
☐ DESERT	☐ TUNDRA
☐ FRESHWATER	☐ MARINE

TYPE

SHAPE

WEIGHT

COLORS

TEXTURE

LUSTER

SKETCH / SAMPLE

LENGTH	WIDTH	DEPTH

EQUIPMENT

-
-
-

SETTINGS

EXTENDED DESCRIPTION

DATE		SKETCH / SAMPLE

DATE

TIME

LOCATION

ENVIRONMENT

☐ FOREST	☐ GRASSLAND
☐ DESERT	☐ TUNDRA
☐ FRESHWATER	☐ MARINE

TYPE

SHAPE

WEIGHT

COLORS

TEXTURE

LUSTER

SKETCH / SAMPLE

LENGTH	WIDTH	DEPTH

EQUIPMENT

-
-
-

SETTINGS

EXTENDED DESCRIPTION

DATE

TIME

LOCATION

ENVIRONMENT

☐ FOREST	☐ GRASSLAND
☐ DESERT	☐ TUNDRA
☐ FRESHWATER	☐ MARINE

TYPE

SHAPE

WEIGHT

COLORS

TEXTURE

LUSTER

SKETCH / SAMPLE

LENGTH	WIDTH	DEPTH

EQUIPMENT

-
-
-

⚙ SETTINGS

EXTENDED DESCRIPTION

DATE	
TIME	
LOCATION	

ENVIRONMENT

☐ FOREST	☐ GRASSLAND
☐ DESERT	☐ TUNDRA
☐ FRESHWATER	☐ MARINE

TYPE	
SHAPE	
WEIGHT	

SKETCH / SAMPLE

LENGTH	WIDTH	DEPTH

COLORS
TEXTURE
LUSTER

EQUIPMENT

-
-
-

SETTINGS

EXTENDED DESCRIPTION

DATE	
TIME	
LOCATION	

ENVIRONMENT

☐ FOREST	☐ GRASSLAND
☐ DESERT	☐ TUNDRA
☐ FRESHWATER	☐ MARINE

TYPE	
SHAPE	
WEIGHT	

SKETCH / SAMPLE

LENGTH	WIDTH	DEPTH

COLORS	
TEXTURE	
LUSTER	

EQUIPMENT

-
-
-

SETTINGS

EXTENDED DESCRIPTION

📅 **DATE**	
🕐 **TIME**	
📍 **LOCATION**	

ENVIRONMENT

☐	FOREST	☐	GRASSLAND
☐	DESERT	☐	TUNDRA
☐	FRESHWATER	☐	MARINE

△ **TYPE**	
▽ **SHAPE**	
⚖ **WEIGHT**	

SKETCH / SAMPLE

LENGTH	WIDTH	DEPTH

◎ **COLORS**	
▨ **TEXTURE**	
✦ **LUSTER**	

EQUIPMENT

- •
- •
- •

⚙ SETTINGS

EXTENDED DESCRIPTION

DATE

TIME

LOCATION

ENVIRONMENT

☐ FOREST	☐ GRASSLAND
☐ DESERT	☐ TUNDRA
☐ FRESHWATER	☐ MARINE

TYPE

SHAPE

WEIGHT

COLORS

TEXTURE

LUSTER

SKETCH / SAMPLE

LENGTH	WIDTH	DEPTH

EQUIPMENT

-
-
-

SETTINGS

EXTENDED DESCRIPTION

DATE

TIME

LOCATION

ENVIRONMENT

☐ FOREST	☐ GRASSLAND
☐ DESERT	☐ TUNDRA
☐ FRESHWATER	☐ MARINE

TYPE

SHAPE

WEIGHT

COLORS

TEXTURE

LUSTER

SKETCH / SAMPLE

LENGTH	WIDTH	DEPTH

EQUIPMENT

- •
- •
- •

SETTINGS

EXTENDED DESCRIPTION

DATE

TIME

LOCATION

ENVIRONMENT

☐ FOREST	☐ GRASSLAND
☐ DESERT	☐ TUNDRA
☐ FRESHWATER	☐ MARINE

TYPE

SHAPE

WEIGHT

COLORS

TEXTURE

LUSTER

SKETCH / SAMPLE

LENGTH	WIDTH	DEPTH

EQUIPMENT

-
-
-

SETTINGS

EXTENDED DESCRIPTION

DATE	
TIME	
LOCATION	

ENVIRONMENT

☐ FOREST	☐ GRASSLAND
☐ DESERT	☐ TUNDRA
☐ FRESHWATER	☐ MARINE

TYPE	
SHAPE	
WEIGHT	

COLORS	
TEXTURE	
LUSTER	

SKETCH / SAMPLE

LENGTH	WIDTH	DEPTH

EQUIPMENT

-
-
-

SETTINGS

EXTENDED DESCRIPTION

DATE	
TIME	
LOCATION	

ENVIRONMENT

☐ FOREST	☐ GRASSLAND
☐ DESERT	☐ TUNDRA
☐ FRESHWATER	☐ MARINE

TYPE	
SHAPE	
WEIGHT	

SKETCH / SAMPLE

LENGTH	WIDTH	DEPTH

COLORS

TEXTURE

LUSTER

EQUIPMENT

-
-
-

SETTINGS

EXTENDED DESCRIPTION

DATE

TIME

LOCATION

ENVIRONMENT

☐ FOREST	☐ GRASSLAND
☐ DESERT	☐ TUNDRA
☐ FRESHWATER	☐ MARINE

TYPE

SHAPE

WEIGHT

COLORS

TEXTURE

LUSTER

SKETCH / SAMPLE

LENGTH	WIDTH	DEPTH

EQUIPMENT

-
-
-

SETTINGS

EXTENDED DESCRIPTION

DATE

TIME

LOCATION

ENVIRONMENT

☐ FOREST	☐ GRASSLAND
☐ DESERT	☐ TUNDRA
☐ FRESHWATER	☐ MARINE

TYPE

SHAPE

WEIGHT

COLORS

TEXTURE

LUSTER

SKETCH / SAMPLE

LENGTH	WIDTH	DEPTH

EQUIPMENT

-
-
-

SETTINGS

EXTENDED DESCRIPTION

DATE

TIME

LOCATION

ENVIRONMENT

☐ FOREST	☐ GRASSLAND
☐ DESERT	☐ TUNDRA
☐ FRESHWATER	☐ MARINE

TYPE

SHAPE

WEIGHT

COLORS

TEXTURE

LUSTER

SKETCH / SAMPLE

LENGTH	WIDTH	DEPTH

EQUIPMENT

-
-
-

SETTINGS

EXTENDED DESCRIPTION

DATE

TIME

LOCATION

ENVIRONMENT

☐ FOREST	☐ GRASSLAND
☐ DESERT	☐ TUNDRA
☐ FRESHWATER	☐ MARINE

TYPE

SHAPE

WEIGHT

COLORS

TEXTURE

LUSTER

SKETCH / SAMPLE

LENGTH	WIDTH	DEPTH

EQUIPMENT

-
-
-

SETTINGS

EXTENDED DESCRIPTION

DATE

TIME

LOCATION

ENVIRONMENT

☐ FOREST	☐ GRASSLAND
☐ DESERT	☐ TUNDRA
☐ FRESHWATER	☐ MARINE

TYPE

SHAPE

WEIGHT

COLORS

TEXTURE

LUSTER

SKETCH / SAMPLE

LENGTH	WIDTH	DEPTH

EQUIPMENT

-
-
-

SETTINGS

EXTENDED DESCRIPTION

DATE

TIME

LOCATION

ENVIRONMENT

☐ FOREST	☐ GRASSLAND
☐ DESERT	☐ TUNDRA
☐ FRESHWATER	☐ MARINE

TYPE

SHAPE

WEIGHT

COLORS

TEXTURE

LUSTER

SKETCH / SAMPLE

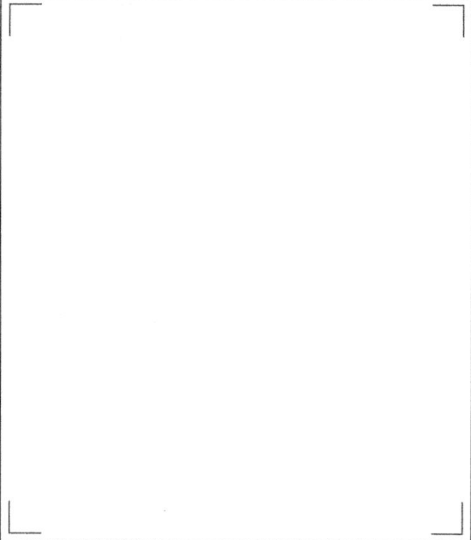

LENGTH	WIDTH	DEPTH

EQUIPMENT

-
-
-

⚬ SETTINGS

EXTENDED DESCRIPTION

DATE

TIME

LOCATION

ENVIRONMENT

☐ FOREST	☐ GRASSLAND
☐ DESERT	☐ TUNDRA
☐ FRESHWATER	☐ MARINE

TYPE

SHAPE

WEIGHT

SKETCH / SAMPLE

LENGTH	WIDTH	DEPTH

COLORS

TEXTURE

LUSTER

EQUIPMENT

-
-
-

SETTINGS

EXTENDED DESCRIPTION

DATE	
TIME	
LOCATION	

ENVIRONMENT

☐ FOREST	☐ GRASSLAND
☐ DESERT	☐ TUNDRA
☐ FRESHWATER	☐ MARINE

TYPE
SHAPE
WEIGHT

SKETCH / SAMPLE

LENGTH	WIDTH	DEPTH

COLORS
TEXTURE
LUSTER

EQUIPMENT

-
-
-

⚙ SETTINGS

EXTENDED DESCRIPTION

DATE

TIME

LOCATION

ENVIRONMENT

☐ FOREST	☐ GRASSLAND
☐ DESERT	☐ TUNDRA
☐ FRESHWATER	☐ MARINE

TYPE

SHAPE

WEIGHT

COLORS

TEXTURE

LUSTER

SKETCH / SAMPLE

LENGTH	WIDTH	DEPTH

EQUIPMENT

-
-
-

SETTINGS

EXTENDED DESCRIPTION

DATE	SKETCH / SAMPLE

DATE

TIME

LOCATION

ENVIRONMENT

☐ FOREST	☐ GRASSLAND
☐ DESERT	☐ TUNDRA
☐ FRESHWATER	☐ MARINE

TYPE

SHAPE

WEIGHT

SKETCH / SAMPLE

LENGTH	WIDTH	DEPTH

COLORS

TEXTURE

LUSTER

EQUIPMENT

-
-
-

SETTINGS

EXTENDED DESCRIPTION

DATE

TIME

LOCATION

ENVIRONMENT

☐ FOREST	☐ GRASSLAND
☐ DESERT	☐ TUNDRA
☐ FRESHWATER	☐ MARINE

TYPE

SHAPE

WEIGHT

COLORS

TEXTURE

LUSTER

SKETCH / SAMPLE

LENGTH	WIDTH	DEPTH

EQUIPMENT

-
-
-

SETTINGS

EXTENDED DESCRIPTION

DATE

TIME

LOCATION

ENVIRONMENT

☐ FOREST	☐ GRASSLAND
☐ DESERT	☐ TUNDRA
☐ FRESHWATER	☐ MARINE

TYPE

SHAPE

WEIGHT

COLORS

TEXTURE

LUSTER

SKETCH / SAMPLE

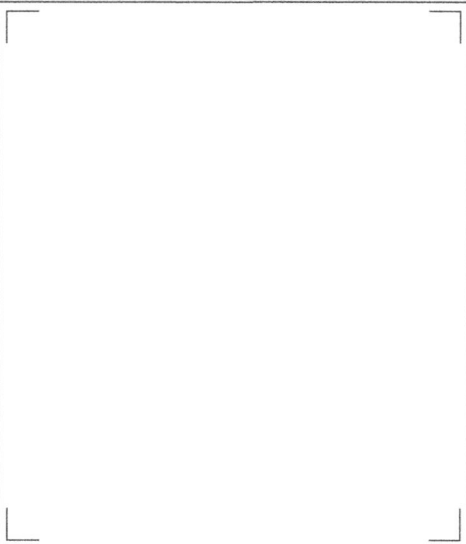

LENGTH	WIDTH	DEPTH

EQUIPMENT

-
-
-

SETTINGS

EXTENDED DESCRIPTION

DATE

TIME

LOCATION

ENVIRONMENT

☐ FOREST	☐ GRASSLAND
☐ DESERT	☐ TUNDRA
☐ FRESHWATER	☐ MARINE

TYPE

SHAPE

WEIGHT

COLORS

TEXTURE

LUSTER

SKETCH / SAMPLE

LENGTH	WIDTH	DEPTH

EQUIPMENT

-
-
-

SETTINGS

EXTENDED DESCRIPTION

DATE	
TIME	
LOCATION	

SKETCH / SAMPLE

LENGTH	WIDTH	DEPTH

ENVIRONMENT

FOREST	GRASSLAND
DESERT	TUNDRA
FRESHWATER	MARINE

TYPE	
SHAPE	
WEIGHT	

COLORS

TEXTURE

LUSTER

EQUIPMENT

-
-
-

SETTINGS

EXTENDED DESCRIPTION

DATE

TIME

LOCATION

ENVIRONMENT

☐ FOREST	☐ GRASSLAND
☐ DESERT	☐ TUNDRA
☐ FRESHWATER	☐ MARINE

TYPE

SHAPE

WEIGHT

COLORS

TEXTURE

LUSTER

SKETCH / SAMPLE

LENGTH	WIDTH	DEPTH

EQUIPMENT

-
-
-

SETTINGS

EXTENDED DESCRIPTION

DATE

TIME

LOCATION

ENVIRONMENT

☐ FOREST	☐ GRASSLAND
☐ DESERT	☐ TUNDRA
☐ FRESHWATER	☐ MARINE

TYPE

SHAPE

WEIGHT

COLORS

TEXTURE

LUSTER

SKETCH / SAMPLE

LENGTH	WIDTH	DEPTH

EQUIPMENT

-
-
-

SETTINGS

EXTENDED DESCRIPTION

DATE

TIME

LOCATION

ENVIRONMENT

☐ FOREST	☐ GRASSLAND
☐ DESERT	☐ TUNDRA
☐ FRESHWATER	☐ MARINE

TYPE

SHAPE

WEIGHT

COLORS

TEXTURE

LUSTER

SKETCH / SAMPLE

LENGTH	WIDTH	DEPTH

EQUIPMENT

-
-
-

SETTINGS

EXTENDED DESCRIPTION

DATE
TIME
LOCATION

ENVIRONMENT

☐ FOREST	☐ GRASSLAND
☐ DESERT	☐ TUNDRA
☐ FRESHWATER	☐ MARINE

TYPE
SHAPE
WEIGHT

SKETCH / SAMPLE

LENGTH	WIDTH	DEPTH

COLORS
TEXTURE
LUSTER

EQUIPMENT

-
-
-

SETTINGS

EXTENDED DESCRIPTION

📅 DATE	
🕐 TIME	
📍 LOCATION	

ENVIRONMENT

☐ FOREST	☐ GRASSLAND
☐ DESERT	☐ TUNDRA
☐ FRESHWATER	☐ MARINE

◈ TYPE	
▽ SHAPE	
🔲 WEIGHT	

SKETCH / SAMPLE

LENGTH	WIDTH	DEPTH

⊛ COLORS	
▨ TEXTURE	
✦ LUSTER	

EQUIPMENT

- •
- •
- •

⚙ SETTINGS

EXTENDED DESCRIPTION

DATE		**SKETCH / SAMPLE**
TIME		
LOCATION		

ENVIRONMENT

☐ FOREST	☐ GRASSLAND
☐ DESERT	☐ TUNDRA
☐ FRESHWATER	☐ MARINE

TYPE

SHAPE

WEIGHT

LENGTH	WIDTH	DEPTH

COLORS

TEXTURE

LUSTER

EQUIPMENT

-
-
-

⚙ SETTINGS

EXTENDED DESCRIPTION

DATE	
TIME	
LOCATION	

ENVIRONMENT

☐ FOREST	☐ GRASSLAND
☐ DESERT	☐ TUNDRA
☐ FRESHWATER	☐ MARINE

TYPE	
SHAPE	
WEIGHT	

SKETCH / SAMPLE

LENGTH	WIDTH	DEPTH

COLORS

TEXTURE

LUSTER

EQUIPMENT

- •
- •
- •

SETTINGS

EXTENDED DESCRIPTION

DATE

TIME

LOCATION

ENVIRONMENT

☐ FOREST	☐ GRASSLAND
☐ DESERT	☐ TUNDRA
☐ FRESHWATER	☐ MARINE

TYPE

SHAPE

WEIGHT

COLORS

TEXTURE

LUSTER

SKETCH / SAMPLE

LENGTH	WIDTH	DEPTH

EQUIPMENT

-
-
-

SETTINGS

EXTENDED DESCRIPTION

DATE	
TIME	
LOCATION	

ENVIRONMENT

☐ FOREST	☐ GRASSLAND
☐ DESERT	☐ TUNDRA
☐ FRESHWATER	☐ MARINE

TYPE	
SHAPE	
WEIGHT	

SKETCH / SAMPLE

LENGTH	WIDTH	DEPTH

COLORS	
TEXTURE	
LUSTER	

EQUIPMENT

-
-
-

SETTINGS

EXTENDED DESCRIPTION

DATE

TIME

LOCATION

ENVIRONMENT

☐ FOREST	☐ GRASSLAND
☐ DESERT	☐ TUNDRA
☐ FRESHWATER	☐ MARINE

TYPE

SHAPE

WEIGHT

COLORS

TEXTURE

LUSTER

SKETCH / SAMPLE

LENGTH	WIDTH	DEPTH

EQUIPMENT

-
-
-

SETTINGS

EXTENDED DESCRIPTION

📅 DATE	
🕐 TIME	
📍 LOCATION	

ENVIRONMENT

☐ FOREST	☐ GRASSLAND
☐ DESERT	☐ TUNDRA
☐ FRESHWATER	☐ MARINE

🔺 TYPE	
🔻 SHAPE	
⚖️ WEIGHT	

◉ COLORS
🖌️ TEXTURE
✦ LUSTER

SKETCH / SAMPLE

LENGTH	WIDTH	DEPTH

EQUIPMENT

- •
- •
- •

⚙️ SETTINGS

EXTENDED DESCRIPTION

DATE

TIME

LOCATION

ENVIRONMENT

☐ FOREST	☐ GRASSLAND
☐ DESERT	☐ TUNDRA
☐ FRESHWATER	☐ MARINE

TYPE

SHAPE

WEIGHT

COLORS

TEXTURE

LUSTER

SKETCH / SAMPLE

LENGTH	WIDTH	DEPTH

EQUIPMENT

-
-
-

SETTINGS

EXTENDED DESCRIPTION

DATE

TIME

LOCATION

ENVIRONMENT

☐ FOREST	☐ GRASSLAND
☐ DESERT	☐ TUNDRA
☐ FRESHWATER	☐ MARINE

TYPE

SHAPE

WEIGHT

COLORS

TEXTURE

LUSTER

SKETCH / SAMPLE

LENGTH	WIDTH	DEPTH

EQUIPMENT

- •
- •
- •

SETTINGS

EXTENDED DESCRIPTION

DATE

TIME

LOCATION

ENVIRONMENT

☐ FOREST	☐ GRASSLAND
☐ DESERT	☐ TUNDRA
☐ FRESHWATER	☐ MARINE

TYPE

SHAPE

WEIGHT

COLORS

TEXTURE

LUSTER

SKETCH / SAMPLE

LENGTH	WIDTH	DEPTH

EQUIPMENT

-
-
-

SETTINGS

EXTENDED DESCRIPTION

DATE	
TIME	
LOCATION	

SKETCH / SAMPLE

LENGTH	WIDTH	DEPTH

ENVIRONMENT

FOREST	GRASSLAND
DESERT	TUNDRA
FRESHWATER	MARINE

TYPE	
SHAPE	
WEIGHT	

COLORS

TEXTURE

LUSTER

EQUIPMENT

-
-
-

SETTINGS

EXTENDED DESCRIPTION

DATE

TIME

LOCATION

ENVIRONMENT

FOREST	GRASSLAND
☐ FOREST	☐ GRASSLAND
☐ DESERT	☐ TUNDRA
☐ FRESHWATER	☐ MARINE

TYPE

SHAPE

WEIGHT

COLORS

TEXTURE

LUSTER

SKETCH / SAMPLE

LENGTH	WIDTH	DEPTH

EQUIPMENT

-
-
-

SETTINGS

EXTENDED DESCRIPTION

DATE

TIME

LOCATION

ENVIRONMENT

☐ FOREST	☐ GRASSLAND
☐ DESERT	☐ TUNDRA
☐ FRESHWATER	☐ MARINE

TYPE

SHAPE

WEIGHT

COLORS

TEXTURE

LUSTER

SKETCH / SAMPLE

LENGTH	WIDTH	DEPTH

EQUIPMENT

-
-
-

SETTINGS

EXTENDED DESCRIPTION

DATE

TIME

LOCATION

ENVIRONMENT

☐ FOREST	☐ GRASSLAND
☐ DESERT	☐ TUNDRA
☐ FRESHWATER	☐ MARINE

TYPE

SHAPE

WEIGHT

COLORS

TEXTURE

LUSTER

SKETCH / SAMPLE

LENGTH	WIDTH	DEPTH

EQUIPMENT

-
-
-

SETTINGS

EXTENDED DESCRIPTION

DATE	SKETCH / SAMPLE
TIME	
LOCATION	

ENVIRONMENT

☐ FOREST	☐ GRASSLAND
☐ DESERT	☐ TUNDRA
☐ FRESHWATER	☐ MARINE

- TYPE
- SHAPE
- WEIGHT

LENGTH	WIDTH	DEPTH

COLORS

TEXTURE

LUSTER

EQUIPMENT

-
-
-

SETTINGS

EXTENDED DESCRIPTION

DATE

TIME

LOCATION

ENVIRONMENT

☐ FOREST	☐ GRASSLAND
☐ DESERT	☐ TUNDRA
☐ FRESHWATER	☐ MARINE

TYPE

SHAPE

WEIGHT

COLORS

TEXTURE

LUSTER

SKETCH / SAMPLE

LENGTH	WIDTH	DEPTH

EQUIPMENT

-
-
-

SETTINGS

EXTENDED DESCRIPTION

DATE	
TIME	
LOCATION	

ENVIRONMENT

☐ FOREST	☐ GRASSLAND
☐ DESERT	☐ TUNDRA
☐ FRESHWATER	☐ MARINE

TYPE	
SHAPE	
WEIGHT	

COLORS
TEXTURE
LUSTER

SKETCH / SAMPLE

LENGTH	WIDTH	DEPTH

EQUIPMENT

-
-
-

SETTINGS

EXTENDED DESCRIPTION

DATE	
TIME	
LOCATION	

SKETCH / SAMPLE

LENGTH	WIDTH	DEPTH

ENVIRONMENT

☐ FOREST	☐ GRASSLAND
☐ DESERT	☐ TUNDRA
☐ FRESHWATER	☐ MARINE

TYPE	
SHAPE	
WEIGHT	

COLORS
TEXTURE
LUSTER

EQUIPMENT

-
-
-

SETTINGS

EXTENDED DESCRIPTION

DATE

TIME

LOCATION

ENVIRONMENT

☐ FOREST	☐ GRASSLAND
☐ DESERT	☐ TUNDRA
☐ FRESHWATER	☐ MARINE

TYPE

SHAPE

WEIGHT

SKETCH / SAMPLE

LENGTH	WIDTH	DEPTH

COLORS

TEXTURE

LUSTER

EQUIPMENT

-
-
-

SETTINGS

EXTENDED DESCRIPTION

DATE

TIME

LOCATION

ENVIRONMENT

☐ FOREST	☐ GRASSLAND
☐ DESERT	☐ TUNDRA
☐ FRESHWATER	☐ MARINE

TYPE

SHAPE

WEIGHT

COLORS

TEXTURE

LUSTER

SKETCH / SAMPLE

LENGTH	WIDTH	DEPTH

EQUIPMENT

-
-
-

SETTINGS

EXTENDED DESCRIPTION

DATE

TIME

LOCATION

ENVIRONMENT

☐ FOREST	☐ GRASSLAND
☐ DESERT	☐ TUNDRA
☐ FRESHWATER	☐ MARINE

TYPE

SHAPE

WEIGHT

COLORS

TEXTURE

LUSTER

SKETCH / SAMPLE

LENGTH	WIDTH	DEPTH

EQUIPMENT

-
-
-

SETTINGS

EXTENDED DESCRIPTION

DATE

TIME

LOCATION

ENVIRONMENT

☐ FOREST	☐ GRASSLAND
☐ DESERT	☐ TUNDRA
☐ FRESHWATER	☐ MARINE

TYPE

SHAPE

WEIGHT

COLORS

TEXTURE

LUSTER

SKETCH / SAMPLE

LENGTH	WIDTH	DEPTH

EQUIPMENT

-
-
-

SETTINGS

EXTENDED DESCRIPTION

DATE

TIME

LOCATION

ENVIRONMENT

☐ FOREST	☐ GRASSLAND
☐ DESERT	☐ TUNDRA
☐ FRESHWATER	☐ MARINE

TYPE

SHAPE

WEIGHT

COLORS

TEXTURE

LUSTER

SKETCH / SAMPLE

LENGTH	WIDTH	DEPTH

EQUIPMENT

-
-
-

SETTINGS

EXTENDED DESCRIPTION

DATE

TIME

LOCATION

ENVIRONMENT

FOREST	GRASSLAND
DESERT	TUNDRA
FRESHWATER	MARINE

TYPE

SHAPE

WEIGHT

COLORS

TEXTURE

LUSTER

SKETCH / SAMPLE

LENGTH	WIDTH	DEPTH

EQUIPMENT

-
-
-

SETTINGS

EXTENDED DESCRIPTION

DATE

TIME

LOCATION

ENVIRONMENT

☐	FOREST	☐	GRASSLAND
☐	DESERT	☐	TUNDRA
☐	FRESHWATER	☐	MARINE

TYPE

SHAPE

WEIGHT

COLORS

TEXTURE

LUSTER

SKETCH / SAMPLE

LENGTH	WIDTH	DEPTH

EQUIPMENT

-
-
-

SETTINGS

EXTENDED DESCRIPTION

DATE

TIME

LOCATION

ENVIRONMENT

☐ FOREST	☐ GRASSLAND
☐ DESERT	☐ TUNDRA
☐ FRESHWATER	☐ MARINE

TYPE

SHAPE

WEIGHT

COLORS

TEXTURE

LUSTER

SKETCH / SAMPLE

LENGTH	WIDTH	DEPTH

EQUIPMENT

-
-
-

SETTINGS

EXTENDED DESCRIPTION

DATE

TIME

LOCATION

ENVIRONMENT

☐ FOREST	☐ GRASSLAND
☐ DESERT	☐ TUNDRA
☐ FRESHWATER	☐ MARINE

TYPE

SHAPE

WEIGHT

COLORS

TEXTURE

LUSTER

SKETCH / SAMPLE

LENGTH	WIDTH	DEPTH

EQUIPMENT

-
-
-

SETTINGS

EXTENDED DESCRIPTION

DATE

TIME

LOCATION

ENVIRONMENT

☐ FOREST	☐ GRASSLAND
☐ DESERT	☐ TUNDRA
☐ FRESHWATER	☐ MARINE

TYPE

SHAPE

WEIGHT

COLORS

TEXTURE

LUSTER

SKETCH / SAMPLE

LENGTH	WIDTH	DEPTH

EQUIPMENT

-
-
-

SETTINGS

EXTENDED DESCRIPTION

DATE

TIME

LOCATION

ENVIRONMENT

☐ FOREST	☐ GRASSLAND
☐ DESERT	☐ TUNDRA
☐ FRESHWATER	☐ MARINE

TYPE

SHAPE

WEIGHT

COLORS

TEXTURE

LUSTER

SKETCH / SAMPLE

LENGTH	WIDTH	DEPTH

EQUIPMENT

-
-
-

SETTINGS

EXTENDED DESCRIPTION

DATE

TIME

LOCATION

ENVIRONMENT	
☐ FOREST	☐ GRASSLAND
☐ DESERT	☐ TUNDRA
☐ FRESHWATER	☐ MARINE

TYPE

SHAPE

WEIGHT

COLORS

TEXTURE

LUSTER

SKETCH / SAMPLE

LENGTH	WIDTH	DEPTH

EQUIPMENT

-
-
-

SETTINGS

EXTENDED DESCRIPTION

DATE

TIME

LOCATION

ENVIRONMENT

☐ FOREST	☐ GRASSLAND
☐ DESERT	☐ TUNDRA
☐ FRESHWATER	☐ MARINE

TYPE

SHAPE

WEIGHT

COLORS

TEXTURE

LUSTER

SKETCH / SAMPLE

LENGTH	WIDTH	DEPTH

EQUIPMENT

-
-
-

SETTINGS

EXTENDED DESCRIPTION

DATE

TIME

LOCATION

ENVIRONMENT

☐ FOREST	☐ GRASSLAND
☐ DESERT	☐ TUNDRA
☐ FRESHWATER	☐ MARINE

TYPE

SHAPE

WEIGHT

COLORS

TEXTURE

LUSTER

SKETCH / SAMPLE

LENGTH	WIDTH	DEPTH

EQUIPMENT

-
-
-

SETTINGS

EXTENDED DESCRIPTION

DATE

TIME

LOCATION

ENVIRONMENT

☐ FOREST	☐ GRASSLAND
☐ DESERT	☐ TUNDRA
☐ FRESHWATER	☐ MARINE

TYPE

SHAPE

WEIGHT

COLORS

TEXTURE

LUSTER

SKETCH / SAMPLE

LENGTH	WIDTH	DEPTH

EQUIPMENT

-
-
-

SETTINGS

EXTENDED DESCRIPTION

DATE

TIME

LOCATION

ENVIRONMENT

☐ FOREST	☐ GRASSLAND
☐ DESERT	☐ TUNDRA
☐ FRESHWATER	☐ MARINE

TYPE

SHAPE

WEIGHT

COLORS

TEXTURE

LUSTER

SKETCH / SAMPLE

LENGTH	WIDTH	DEPTH

EQUIPMENT

-
-
-

SETTINGS

EXTENDED DESCRIPTION

DATE

TIME

LOCATION

ENVIRONMENT

☐ FOREST	☐ GRASSLAND
☐ DESERT	☐ TUNDRA
☐ FRESHWATER	☐ MARINE

TYPE

SHAPE

WEIGHT

COLORS

TEXTURE

LUSTER

SKETCH / SAMPLE

LENGTH	WIDTH	DEPTH

EQUIPMENT

-
-
-

SETTINGS

EXTENDED DESCRIPTION

DATE		
TIME		
LOCATION		

SKETCH / SAMPLE

LENGTH	WIDTH	DEPTH

ENVIRONMENT

☐ FOREST	☐ GRASSLAND
☐ DESERT	☐ TUNDRA
☐ FRESHWATER	☐ MARINE

TYPE	
SHAPE	
WEIGHT	

COLORS

TEXTURE

LUSTER

EQUIPMENT

-
-
-

SETTINGS

EXTENDED DESCRIPTION

DATE	
TIME	
LOCATION	

SKETCH / SAMPLE

LENGTH	WIDTH	DEPTH

ENVIRONMENT

FOREST	GRASSLAND
DESERT	TUNDRA
FRESHWATER	MARINE

TYPE	
SHAPE	
WEIGHT	

COLORS	
TEXTURE	
LUSTER	

EQUIPMENT

-
-
-

SETTINGS

EXTENDED DESCRIPTION

DATE

TIME

LOCATION

ENVIRONMENT

☐ FOREST	☐ GRASSLAND
☐ DESERT	☐ TUNDRA
☐ FRESHWATER	☐ MARINE

TYPE

SHAPE

WEIGHT

COLORS

TEXTURE

LUSTER

SKETCH / SAMPLE

LENGTH	WIDTH	DEPTH

EQUIPMENT

-
-
-

SETTINGS

EXTENDED DESCRIPTION

DATE	
TIME	
LOCATION	

SKETCH / SAMPLE

LENGTH	WIDTH	DEPTH

ENVIRONMENT

☐ FOREST	☐ GRASSLAND
☐ DESERT	☐ TUNDRA
☐ FRESHWATER	☐ MARINE

TYPE	
SHAPE	
WEIGHT	

COLORS

TEXTURE

LUSTER

EQUIPMENT

- •
- •
- •

SETTINGS

EXTENDED DESCRIPTION

DATE

TIME

LOCATION

SKETCH / SAMPLE

LENGTH	WIDTH	DEPTH

ENVIRONMENT

☐ FOREST	☐ GRASSLAND
☐ DESERT	☐ TUNDRA
☐ FRESHWATER	☐ MARINE

TYPE

SHAPE

WEIGHT

COLORS

TEXTURE

LUSTER

EQUIPMENT

-
-
-

SETTINGS

EXTENDED DESCRIPTION

DATE

TIME

LOCATION

ENVIRONMENT

☐ FOREST	☐ GRASSLAND
☐ DESERT	☐ TUNDRA
☐ FRESHWATER	☐ MARINE

TYPE

SHAPE

WEIGHT

COLORS

TEXTURE

LUSTER

SKETCH / SAMPLE

LENGTH	WIDTH	DEPTH

EQUIPMENT

-
-
-

SETTINGS

EXTENDED DESCRIPTION

DATE	
TIME	
LOCATION	

ENVIRONMENT

☐ FOREST	☐ GRASSLAND
☐ DESERT	☐ TUNDRA
☐ FRESHWATER	☐ MARINE

TYPE	
SHAPE	
WEIGHT	

SKETCH / SAMPLE

LENGTH	WIDTH	DEPTH

COLORS
TEXTURE
LUSTER

EQUIPMENT

-
-
-

SETTINGS

EXTENDED DESCRIPTION

DATE

TIME

LOCATION

ENVIRONMENT

☐ FOREST	☐ GRASSLAND
☐ DESERT	☐ TUNDRA
☐ FRESHWATER	☐ MARINE

TYPE

SHAPE

WEIGHT

SKETCH / SAMPLE

LENGTH	WIDTH	DEPTH

COLORS

TEXTURE

LUSTER

EQUIPMENT

-
-
-

SETTINGS

EXTENDED DESCRIPTION

DATE

TIME

LOCATION

ENVIRONMENT

☐ FOREST	☐ GRASSLAND
☐ DESERT	☐ TUNDRA
☐ FRESHWATER	☐ MARINE

TYPE

SHAPE

WEIGHT

COLORS

TEXTURE

LUSTER

SKETCH / SAMPLE

LENGTH	WIDTH	DEPTH

EQUIPMENT

-
-
-

SETTINGS

EXTENDED DESCRIPTION

DATE

TIME

LOCATION

ENVIRONMENT

☐ FOREST	☐ GRASSLAND
☐ DESERT	☐ TUNDRA
☐ FRESHWATER	☐ MARINE

TYPE

SHAPE

WEIGHT

COLORS

TEXTURE

LUSTER

SKETCH / SAMPLE

LENGTH	WIDTH	DEPTH

EQUIPMENT

-
-
-

SETTINGS

EXTENDED DESCRIPTION

DATE

TIME

LOCATION

ENVIRONMENT

☐ FOREST	☐ GRASSLAND
☐ DESERT	☐ TUNDRA
☐ FRESHWATER	☐ MARINE

TYPE

SHAPE

WEIGHT

COLORS

TEXTURE

LUSTER

SKETCH / SAMPLE

LENGTH	WIDTH	DEPTH

EQUIPMENT

-
-
-

⚬ SETTINGS

EXTENDED DESCRIPTION

DATE

TIME

LOCATION

ENVIRONMENT

☐ FOREST	☐ GRASSLAND
☐ DESERT	☐ TUNDRA
☐ FRESHWATER	☐ MARINE

TYPE

SHAPE

WEIGHT

COLORS

TEXTURE

LUSTER

SKETCH / SAMPLE

LENGTH	WIDTH	DEPTH

EQUIPMENT

-
-
-

SETTINGS

EXTENDED DESCRIPTION

DATE	
TIME	
LOCATION	

ENVIRONMENT

☐ FOREST	☐ GRASSLAND
☐ DESERT	☐ TUNDRA
☐ FRESHWATER	☐ MARINE

TYPE	
SHAPE	
WEIGHT	

SKETCH / SAMPLE

LENGTH	WIDTH	DEPTH

COLORS

TEXTURE

LUSTER

EQUIPMENT

-
-
-

SETTINGS

EXTENDED DESCRIPTION

DATE

TIME

LOCATION

ENVIRONMENT

☐ FOREST	☐ GRASSLAND
☐ DESERT	☐ TUNDRA
☐ FRESHWATER	☐ MARINE

TYPE

SHAPE

WEIGHT

COLORS

TEXTURE

LUSTER

SKETCH / SAMPLE

LENGTH	WIDTH	DEPTH

EQUIPMENT

-
-
-

SETTINGS

EXTENDED DESCRIPTION

DATE

TIME

LOCATION

ENVIRONMENT

☐ FOREST	☐ GRASSLAND
☐ DESERT	☐ TUNDRA
☐ FRESHWATER	☐ MARINE

TYPE

SHAPE

WEIGHT

COLORS

TEXTURE

LUSTER

SKETCH / SAMPLE

LENGTH	WIDTH	DEPTH

EQUIPMENT

-
-
-

⚙ SETTINGS

EXTENDED DESCRIPTION

DATE	
TIME	
LOCATION	

ENVIRONMENT

☐ FOREST	☐ GRASSLAND
☐ DESERT	☐ TUNDRA
☐ FRESHWATER	☐ MARINE

TYPE	
SHAPE	
WEIGHT	

COLORS	
TEXTURE	
LUSTER	

SKETCH / SAMPLE

LENGTH	WIDTH	DEPTH

EQUIPMENT

-
-
-

SETTINGS

EXTENDED DESCRIPTION

DATE

TIME

LOCATION

ENVIRONMENT

☐ FOREST	☐ GRASSLAND
☐ DESERT	☐ TUNDRA
☐ FRESHWATER	☐ MARINE

TYPE

SHAPE

WEIGHT

COLORS

TEXTURE

LUSTER

SKETCH / SAMPLE

LENGTH	WIDTH	DEPTH

EQUIPMENT

-
-
-

SETTINGS

EXTENDED DESCRIPTION

DATE

TIME

LOCATION

ENVIRONMENT

☐ FOREST	☐ GRASSLAND
☐ DESERT	☐ TUNDRA
☐ FRESHWATER	☐ MARINE

TYPE

SHAPE

WEIGHT

COLORS

TEXTURE

LUSTER

SKETCH / SAMPLE

LENGTH	WIDTH	DEPTH

EQUIPMENT

-
-
-

SETTINGS

EXTENDED DESCRIPTION

DATE

| TIME |

| LOCATION |

ENVIRONMENT

☐ FOREST	☐ GRASSLAND
☐ DESERT	☐ TUNDRA
☐ FRESHWATER	☐ MARINE

TYPE
SHAPE
WEIGHT

SKETCH / SAMPLE

LENGTH	WIDTH	DEPTH

COLORS
TEXTURE
LUSTER

EQUIPMENT

•
•
•
SETTINGS

EXTENDED DESCRIPTION

DATE

TIME

LOCATION

ENVIRONMENT

☐ FOREST	☐ GRASSLAND
☐ DESERT	☐ TUNDRA
☐ FRESHWATER	☐ MARINE

TYPE

SHAPE

WEIGHT

COLORS

TEXTURE

LUSTER

SKETCH / SAMPLE

LENGTH	WIDTH	DEPTH

EQUIPMENT

-
-
-

SETTINGS

EXTENDED DESCRIPTION

DATE

TIME

LOCATION

ENVIRONMENT

☐ FOREST	☐ GRASSLAND
☐ DESERT	☐ TUNDRA
☐ FRESHWATER	☐ MARINE

TYPE

SHAPE

WEIGHT

COLORS

TEXTURE

LUSTER

SKETCH / SAMPLE

LENGTH	WIDTH	DEPTH

EQUIPMENT

-
-
-

SETTINGS

EXTENDED DESCRIPTION

DATE

TIME

LOCATION

ENVIRONMENT

☐ FOREST	☐ GRASSLAND
☐ DESERT	☐ TUNDRA
☐ FRESHWATER	☐ MARINE

TYPE

SHAPE

WEIGHT

COLORS

TEXTURE

LUSTER

SKETCH / SAMPLE

LENGTH	WIDTH	DEPTH

EQUIPMENT

-
-
-

SETTINGS

EXTENDED DESCRIPTION

DATE

TIME

LOCATION

ENVIRONMENT

☐ FOREST	☐ GRASSLAND
☐ DESERT	☐ TUNDRA
☐ FRESHWATER	☐ MARINE

TYPE

SHAPE

WEIGHT

SKETCH / SAMPLE

LENGTH	WIDTH	DEPTH

COLORS

TEXTURE

LUSTER

EQUIPMENT

-
-
-

SETTINGS

EXTENDED DESCRIPTION

DATE	SKETCH / SAMPLE
TIME	
LOCATION	

ENVIRONMENT

☐ FOREST	☐ GRASSLAND
☐ DESERT	☐ TUNDRA
☐ FRESHWATER	☐ MARINE

TYPE
SHAPE
WEIGHT

LENGTH	WIDTH	DEPTH

COLORS
TEXTURE
LUSTER

EQUIPMENT

-
-
-

SETTINGS

EXTENDED DESCRIPTION

DATE
TIME
LOCATION

ENVIRONMENT

☐ FOREST	☐ GRASSLAND
☐ DESERT	☐ TUNDRA
☐ FRESHWATER	☐ MARINE

TYPE
SHAPE
WEIGHT

COLORS
TEXTURE
LUSTER

SKETCH / SAMPLE

LENGTH	WIDTH	DEPTH

EQUIPMENT

- •
- •
- •

SETTINGS

EXTENDED DESCRIPTION

DATE

TIME

LOCATION

ENVIRONMENT

☐ FOREST	☐ GRASSLAND
☐ DESERT	☐ TUNDRA
☐ FRESHWATER	☐ MARINE

TYPE

SHAPE

WEIGHT

COLORS

TEXTURE

LUSTER

SKETCH / SAMPLE

LENGTH	WIDTH	DEPTH

EQUIPMENT

-
-
-

SETTINGS

EXTENDED DESCRIPTION

Printed in Great Britain
by Amazon